VULCAN

AEROGUIDE 29: AVRO VULCAN B Mk 2

Roger Chesneau

INTRODUCTION

THE DATE 31 March 1984 truly marked the end of an era for the Royal Air Force, for it was on that day that No 50 Squadron, the last unit to operate the Avro Vulcan, disbanded. Its significance lies in the fact that the retirement of the Vulcan officially signalled the relinquishment of the RAF's capability in the field of long-range strategic bombing—a capability that had its origins in the 'bloody paralysers' of World War I, was nurtured and developed through the 1920s and 1930s, was unleashed to tremendous effect during World War II, and was called upon for the last time in 1982. The wisdom of abandoning what had for over sixty years been a central doctrine in the defence of the realm will no doubt be revealed over the passage of time.

The RAF's association with this majestic aircraft—an association which spanned more than a quarter of a century—thus finally ended, and thereafter only a few Handley Page Victor tankers remained in service as the last reminders of Britain's formidable 'V-bomber' force of the late 1950s and 1960s. Remarkably, however, some twenty Vulcans—a significant percentage of the total production run—exist today, in various states of preservation; three of these are are more than mere static exhibits, and are capable of running their engines and taxying. Such is the affection in which the aircraft is held.

Readers will notice that Vulcan tankers, designated B Mk 2K (though frequently referred to as Vulcan K Mk 2, or simply K.2), feature prominently in the close-up photographs appearing in this volume. However, for all practical purposes these variants of the *genre* were externally distinguishable from the B.2 only by the presence of the refuelling 'skip' beneath the tail fairing, the absence of the cooling intake from the starboard side nearby, and the distinctive high-visiliblity paintwork on the undersurfaces of the aircraft.

For this volume, I acknowledge, with gratitude, the assistance given by the Royal Air Force, in particular by Flt Lt Michael Fogarty, formerly CRO at RAF Waddington; Sqn Ldr Ron Hellen, No 50 Squadron; and Cpl Ray Nightingale, No 50 Squadron. Uncredited photographs throughout the following pages were taken by kind permission of the Officer Commanding, RAF Waddington, and are the copyright of the author and publisher. Thanks are also due to Harry Holmes, formerly of British Aerospace, Woodford, and to the Martin Baker Aircraft Company. For assistance with photographs and information, I am indebted as always to my good friend Dick Ward, and also to Andy Leitch, Paul Hartley and Craig Bulman (author of *The Vulcan B Mk 2 from a Different Angle*); the input from these four gentlemen was at the same time immediate, unstinting and vital. David Griffiths and Charles Toop also assisited with photographs, and thanks go to them.

No book is perfect, and so errors may be found within the following pages. It must be stressed that these are my own responsibility.

R.D.C.

Above (main illustration): XA891, an early Vulcan B Mk 1, in aluminium finish, up for tests in 1955. *BAe*
Far left: Vulcan B Mk 2s on the pan at RAF Scampton, 11 May 1961. *BAe*
Left: Delta take-off. Camouflage was introduced to the Vulcan fleet when the high-altitude nuclear bombing role was abandoned in view of the increasing efficacy of Soviet-bloc AA missiles. *BAe*
Inset: Vulcan production at Avro's Woodford factory. *BAe*

DELTA FORCE

THE closing years of World War II witnessed the introduction of two revolutionary technologies to the concept of military air power—the turbojet and the atomic bomb. By the time hostilities were finally brought to a close, it had become clear that henceforth the strategic bomber—the long-range heavy bomber—would look very different from the Stirlings, Halifaxes and Lancasters which were responsible for conducting the Royal Air Force's offensive against Germany and would, moreover, be called upon to carry weapons thousands of times more destructive. The nuclear role, it was perceived, demanded an aircraft capable of flying great distances, at great speed and at high altitude, in order to frustrate an enemy's attempts at interception (the aircraft would carry no defensive armament); furthermore, atomic devices being weighty affairs in those early days, its weapons bay would need to hold a 10,000lb bomb.

DELTA PLANFORM

Such jolts to what had hitherto been a steady 30-year evolution in heavy bomber development provided aircraft manufacturers with exciting and exacting opportunities for radical designs, and the two aircraft that would in due course be ordered into production in response to Specification B.35/46 of 1 January 1947—the Handley Page HP.80 and the Avro Type 698—were of startlingly different appearance from anything that had gone before. Christened Victor and Vulcan, respectively, they would, together with the less exotic Vickers Valiant, make up the celebrated 'V-bomber' force.

The speed (500kt cruise) required by B.35/46, the range (3000-plus miles), the altitude (50,000ft), the maximum weight (100,000lb, restricted thus by existing military runway dimensions) and the 10,000lb bomb set out the broad parameters of the design: turbojet propulsion to provide the necessary thrust; a swept wing to overcome the compressibility problems afflicting near-sonic flight; sufficient fuel to enable the aircraft to reach its target and return home; a wing of the required size to provide adequate lift at high altitudes; a pressurised compartment to enable the crew to survive at such heights; and a weapons bay of the necessary capacity. From an engineering viewpoint, these conditions in themselves posed no insuperable difficulties: the trick was to achieve something viable within the weight limits.

What eventually emerged from the Avro facility was an aircraft that resembled a flying triangle—a delta planform of immense area in relation to its span. Aerodynamically, it was superbly 'clean' in order to offer minimum drag and thus extract the maximum possible performance; structurally, it was extremely strong, capable of withstanding the rigours imposed by the aircraft's role.

SEVEN-OH-SEVEN

The revolutionary nature of the new bomber—especially in terms of its high speed requirement and its wing geometry—called for a good deal of clear thinking and, indeed, calculated risk, and in order to obtain data it was decided at an early stage to build and fly a number of scaled-down versions, each charged with investigating a particular range of characteristics. The first of these Avro 707s, VX784, was completed in August 1949, but after conducting a small munber of successful test flights it met an early demise when it crashed the following month, killing the pilot. The low-speed capabilities of a delta wing were the province of the 707B, VX790, which first flew a year after its predecessor; high-speed flight investigation was conducted by a 707A, WD280, which appeared in the summer of the following year, 1951; and a further two aircraft joined the trials programme over the next couple of years, another

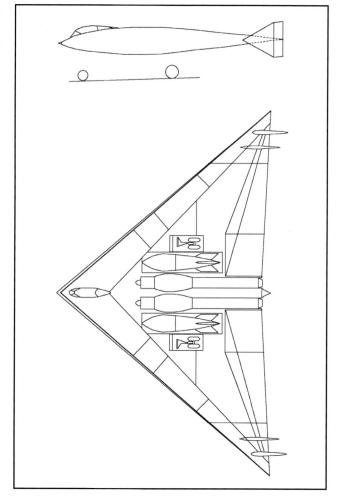

Below: Preliminary design for B.35/46, the specification which would result in the Vulcan bomber. The drawing is based on Avro designer Roy Chadwick's original sketch. *Author*
Right: Avro Type 698 evolution. Dual bomb bays were a feature of the early design sketches. A civil airliner design based on the Type 698—dubbed Avro Atlantic—proved stillborn. *Author*
Far right: General arrangement of the Avro Type 707A. *Author*
Right, centre: The Avro 707B, VX790 (left), showing the dorsal intake that was a feature of this variant. The Type 707C WZ744 (right) was a two-seater and first flew in the summer of 1953. *BAe/Keith McKenzie*
Right, lower: The Avro Type 698—the Vulcan prototype—in 1952. The straight wing leading edges of the original design are clearly seen. *BAe*

4 VULCAN

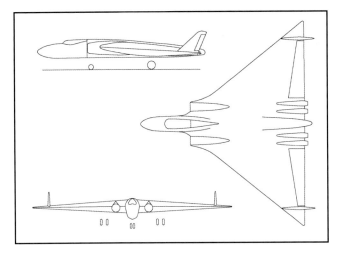
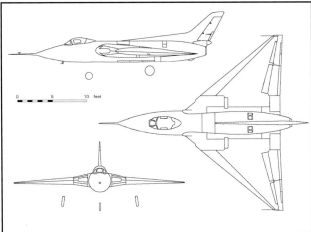

707A (WZ736) and a side-by-side two-seater, 707C WZ744. These aircraft together provided a mass of valuable data and proved the viability of the delta configuration. After the introduction of the Vulcan into service, they went on to conduct research associated with, for example, engine intake turbulence, side-by-side training layouts and delta wing leading-edge geometry (the results of which latter were subsequently applied the Vulcan itself).

MARK 1, MARK 2

The Vulcan protoype flew for the first time on 30 August 1952. It was powered by comparatively low-output (6,500lb thrust) Rolls-Royce Avon RA.3 turbojets owing to the unavailability of the Bristol Olympus, the engine earmarked for service aircraft. It took the Farnborough Air Show by storm a few days later when the test pilot, Wg Cdr Roly Falk, rolled the huge machine before the assembled

spectators. In those far-off, more patriotic days, press coverage of the first public appearance of the Type 698 (as it was still known) was huge, and without exception very positive. Moreover, such was the faith placed in the new bomber that a production contract for 25 examples was awarded to Avro before the first prototype had flown.

A FEW SHORTCOMINGS

The prototype, VX770, was joined almost exactly a year later by a second aircraft, VX777, which was powered by Olympus 100s each offering a fifty per cent increase in thrust, and the two aircraft conducted an intensive series of flight trials over the following months pending the roll-out of the first production Vulcan, XA889, which appeared in January 1955. The trials showed up a number of shortcomings, notably a potential weakness in the outer wing which, in the event of buffeting encountered during high-speed, high-altitude flight, could cause premature fatigue in the structure. Appropriate modifications were made both to VX777 and to the basic design: the first few production B Mk 1s had straight leading edges to the wings, and the rest introduced varying angles along the leading edges; all but one of the earlier Vulcans was retrofitted in this way. In the B Mk 2, first flown in August 1958, this concept was developed further in the design of new, enlarged outer wing panels, principally to bring out the full benefits of the higher-rated Olympus engines now becoming available. Seventy B Mk 1s were ordered, but in the event the final 25 of these were completed to B Mk 2 standards whilst still on the assembly line; and a further 64 new-build B.2s were procured from Avro.

Below left: A B Mk 1 from the first RAF Vulcan unit, No 230 OCU. The shape of the tail fairing changed in later years with the requirement for electronic countermeasures (ECM) equipment. *BAe*
Below right: XA901, another B Mk 1 from No 230 OCU, on approach at Yeadon, June 1960. *Richard L. Ward*
Right, centre: VX777, the second prototype, following the reconstruction of its wing to B.2 standard configuration. The Avro company insignia is carried on the fin. *BAe*
Right, bottom: XH535 served with the A&AEE at Boscombe Down for four years from 1964 before being destroyed in a crash. *BAe*

AVRO VULCAN SPECIFICATIONS

	B Mk 1	B Mk 1A	B Mk 2
Engines	Four Bristol Siddeley Olympus 101 (each rated at 11,000lb), 102 (12,000lb) or 104 (13,500lb)	Four Bristol Siddeley Olympus 104 (each rated at 13,500lb)	Four Bristol Siddeley Olympus 201 or 202 (each rated at 17,000lb) or 301 (20,000lb)
Dimensions			
Length	97ft 1in (29.6m)	99ft 11in (31.1m); 105ft 11in (32.3m) with refuelling probe	99ft 11in (31.1m); 105ft 11in (32.3m) with refuelling probe
Wingspan	99ft (30.2m)	99ft (30.2m)	111ft (33.8m)
Height	26ft 6in (8.1m)	26ft 6in (8.1m)	27ft 2in (8.3m)
Wing area	3,554 sq ft (330.1m^2)	3,554 sq ft (330.1m^2)	3,964 sq ft (368.2m^2)
Take-off weight (max.)	190,000lb (86,167kg)	190,000lb (86,167kg)	204,000lb (92,517kg)
Performance			
Max. speed	625mph (1,000kph) at 36,000ft (11,000m) = Mach 0.92	625mph (1,000kph) at 36,000ft (11,000m) = Mach 0.92	645mph (1,040kph) at 36,000ft (11,000m) = Mach 0.95; in practice, limited to Mach 0.93 (Olympus 201) or Mach 0.92 (301)
Service ceiling	55,000ft (16,750m)	55,000ft (16,750m)	65,000ft (19,800m); in practice imited to 50,000ft (B.2) or 55,000ft (MRR)
Range (typical max.)	3,900 miles (6,300km)	3,900 miles (6,300km)	4,600 miles (7,400km)
Warload	Blue Danube, Violet Club, Mk 5, Red Beard, Yellow Sun Mk 1 or 2 (nuclear); or twenty-one 1,000lb (conventional)	As B Mk1	Yellow Sun Mk 2, Red Beard, WE 177A/B/C (nuclear) or Blue Steel (nuclear); or twenty-one 1,000lb (conventional)

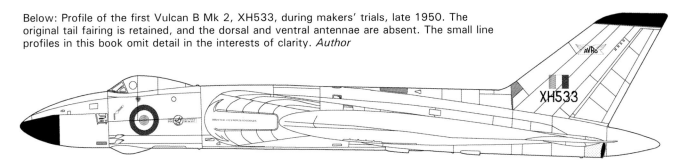

Below: Profile of the first Vulcan B Mk 2, XH533, during makers' trials, late 1950. The original tail fairing is retained, and the dorsal and ventral antennae are absent. The small line profiles in this book omit detail in the interests of clarity. *Author*

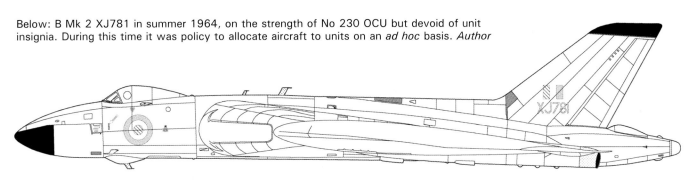

Below: B Mk 2 XJ781 in summer 1964, on the strength of No 230 OCU but devoid of unit insignia. During this time it was policy to allocate aircraft to units on an *ad hoc* basis. *Author*

ENGINE TESTBED

The Vulcan prototypes continued as trials aircraft following the type's service entry in May 1956, the sheer size of the airframe lending itself particularly well for use as an engine testbed. Rolls-Royce Conway turbojets were trialled in VX770 (which crashed as a result of wing failure in 1958—though it was being flown outside the limits at the time), while a production B Mk 1, XA902, was transferred to Rolls-Royce and tested both Conways and Speys. The Olympus engines destined for Concorde and the ill-fated BAC TSR.2 strike bomber, and the RB.199 fitted in the current Tornado, were among other units trialled by Vulcans; in these instances the powerplants were carried externally in aerodynamic packages beneath the fusleage rather than within the wings.

STAND-OFF

VULCAN B Mk 1s had all been phased out of service by the late 1960s, although not before several modifications had been worked into the aircraft. Uprated engines, an electronic countermeasures (ECM) package in a revised tail fairing and the installation of an inflight refuelling system had brought about a redesignation to B Mk 1A. The more powerful B Mk 2 began to supplant the earlier mark towards the end of 1961.

By this time it was becoming evident to the defence establishment that the relative invulnerability of the high-flying, fast jet bomber was being questioned more and more effectively with the advent of potent surface-to-air missiles—dramatically brought home to the West on 1 May 1960 when a Lockheed U-2 reconnaissance aircraft piloted by CIA employee Gary Powers was shot down while overflying the Soviet Union, allegedly by an SA-2 ('Guideline') missile. The incident caused not only a major political row in the continuing 'Cold War' between the Soviet bloc and the West, but, more pragmaticlly, a major re-evaluation of the West's strategic nuclear deterrent. It was claimed that Powers' U-2 had been flying at an altitude of 80,000ft, and the inference was obvious.

BLUE STEEL

In the late 1950s, the United States furnished RAF Bomber Command with seventy-two Mk 5 nuclear weapons, two dozen of which were stored at Waddington; at about this time also, Violet Clubs—Blue Danube casings utilising the new Green Grass 500kt warhead, the latter deveoped for the next-generation Yellow Sun bombs—were made available to the V-bombers at Scampton and Finningley. The U-2 incident, however, gave urgency to the introduction to service of a 'stand-off' nuclear weapon, which could be launched at a distance from its target and thus keep the host aircraft well away from local air defences. The Avro Blue Steel was designed to fit this requirement. It had been ordered as far back as 1956 and was in fact undergoing trials at the time of the U-2 affair. Carried semi-recessed in the bomb bays of both Vulcan and Victor bombers, it entered service in 1962, supplementing the Yellow Sun freefall nuclear weapons now carried by the V-bombers. It constituted Great Britain's strategic nuclear deterrent for the next seven

Above: Freefall nuclear weapons carried by the V-bombers prior to the adoption of Blue Steel included the colossal (10,000lb) Blue Danube (top) and, subsequently, the rather smaller Yellow Sun Mk 1 (centre) and Yellow Sun Mk 2 (bottom). Warhead yields increased progressively—40kt, 500kt and 1Mt, respectively. *Crown Copyright*

Left: An inert Blue Steel on display, the figures at left giving an indication of the weapons's considerable dimensions. *BAe*
Opposite top left: The weapon was borne aloft sem-recessed in the Vulcan's bomb bay. The carrier aircraft here appears to be the B Mk 1 XA903: in service beneath B.2s, the missile fitted against the aircraft more snugly. *BAe*
Opposite top right: Blue Steel mounted on the specially designed AEC Mandator Mk V transporter. *BAe*

8 VULCAN

Below: The B.1 XA903 was engaged is the first airborne trials for Blue Steel and is seen here undergoing systems checks at Avro's Woodford facility. *BAe*

years or so, until the Polaris SLBM, carried by Royal Navy submarines, became fully operational.

Blue Steel, though usually referred to as a 'stand-off bomb', was in effect an air-to-ground missile. Production examples were powered by a 16,000lb thrust Bristol Siddeley Stentor rocket motor. It was designed for launch up to 100 miles from target and at 40,000ft, and on release it would drop several hundred feet before its motor fired. Accelerating to speeds in excess of Mach 2, it zoomed to 70,000ft and then dived on to the target, guided by its inbuilt inertial navigation system, by which time the parent aircraft had turned for home base and, it was hoped, safety. The Red Snow warhead, the same design as that installed in the contemporary Yellow Sun Mk 2 free-fall weapon, was officially, if rather cagily, described as having a yield 'in the megaton range'. The missile was 35ft in length, had a maximum span of 13ft and weighed some 16,000lb. CEP (Circular Error Probability) was by today's standards hardly pinpoint, averaging 400 yards. Fifty-seven production examples (Type W.105) were ordered—48 unit establishment, five backing and four proof rounds—plus sixteen W.103A training rounds. In addition, numerous W.100/100A pre-production and test missiles were made available.

With the phasing out of Blue Steel, all Vulcans reverted to the delivery of nuclear free-fall bombs as their primary role —which, from 1966 onwards, meant carrying the very much smaller though highly versatile WE.177. They could also deliver the 15–25kt Red Beard, which in addition armed tactical aircraft of both the Royal Air Force and the Royal Navy during the 1960s and beyond. The conventional bombing capability was retained though not emphasised—and the Vulcan would be called upon to use it in due course.

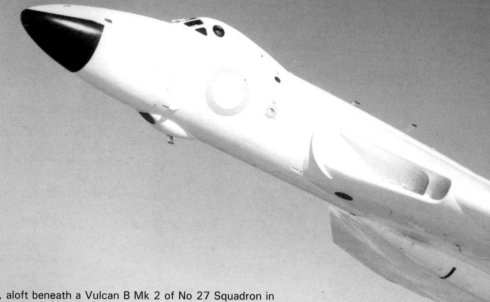

Main picture: Blue Steel in service, aloft beneath a Vulcan B Mk 2 of No 27 Squadron in February 1963 . . . *BAe*
Top right: . . . and another, this time in the tender care of personnel from No 617 Squadron some six months earlier. *BAe*
Below: XH538 and XH539, both early-production B.2s, conducted live-firing trials with Blue Steel over the Woomera test range in Australia. This image, which shows '539, is dated 15 August 1961. *BAe*
Right: XH539 with Blue Steel on landing approach, August 1961. *BAe*

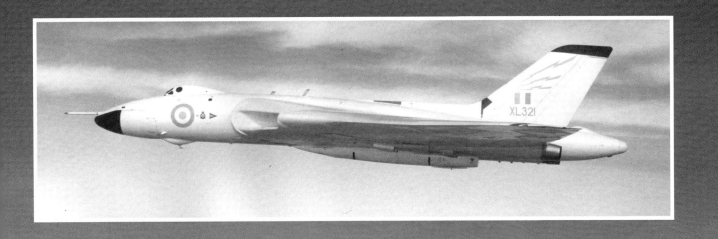

DEAD-ENDS

THE Blue Steel stand-off missile was first mooted in the autumn of 1954, and was ordered into production in March 1956. The gestation period was long and somewhat tortuous, owing mainly to problems with harmonising the new technologies involved, and it was not until more than six years later that the weapon could be made available to the V-bomber squadrons. Enemy air defence technology, needless to say, was also moving along as development work on Blue Steel progressed, but the temptation to tinker with the capability of the missile was resisted and it entered service with its original design requirements more or less intact. A Mk 2 version was studied but abandoned: little is known about this, apart from the fact that it was (reportedly) to be powered by a ramjet, implying much greater stand-off for the carrier aircraft.

GAM-87

One reason for the decision not to proceed with the Mk 2 variant was that, by the late 1950s, the Douglas Aircraft Company had on its drawing boards the GAM-87 Skybolt air-launched ballistic missile (ALBM), capable of carrying a 1.2Mt nuclear weapon across a range of 1,150 miles— a tenfold improvement over Blue Steel's range and representing a commensurate improvement in the chances of bomber crews returning to base unscathed. The Skybolt programme was authorised in 1959 and a US Government contract was awarded the following year, but it was dogged with difficulties, not the least of which were several unsuccessful test flights, and the end result was summary cancellation in December 1962. The British Government was offered the opportunity to continue with the programme, but declined.

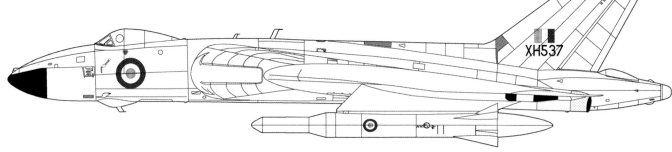

Above: Close view of a dummy Skybolt missile and wing pylon fitted to Vulcan XH537. The aircraft proved eminently suited to the carriage of these weapons. *BAe*

Above: Profile of the Skybolt trials Vulcan XH537. The aircraft was finished in the standard all-white scheme, and the missiles were painted up in sympathy. *Author*
Below: It is not often appreciated that Blue Steel and Skybolt trials were being conducted by Avro almost concurrently: this image of '537 is dated 29 September 1961. *BAe*
Opposite page top: The first Skybolt drop from a Vulcan was made on 1 December 1961. *BAe via Paul Hartley*

Opposite centre: A general arrangement plan of the proposed Vulcan B Mk 3. Up to six Skybolts would constitute the warload, giving the aircraft a truly massive 'punch'. *Author*
Opposite bottom: A simplified general-arrangement plan of the somewhat far-fetched 'Gnat Carrier' proposal. Three of these diminutive fighters, each armed with a nuclear weapon, were shown carried beneath the Vulcan mother aircraft. *Author*

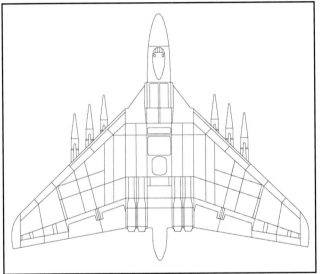

The GAM-87 had an overall length of 38ft 3in, a maximum body diameter of 2ft 11in and an overall span of 5ft 6in. It weighed approximately 11,000lb and on launch would have accelerated to 9,500mph and a maximum altitude of some 300 miles in a ballistic trajectory. Power was provided by an Aerojet General two-stage solid-fuel rocket motor.

One of the Vulcan B Mk 2 trials aircraft, XH557, was selected to conduct tests using dummy Skybolts. The first such flight was made in November 1961 and drops were made, with success, the following month. It was anticipated that an upgraded version of the aicraft, the B Mk 3, would be engineered as a Skybolt launcher for operational purposes, but studies were halted with the cancellation of the Skybolt programme. A projected order for 144 Skybolts for RAF use has been mentioned, with a service entry date of 1966.

NUCLEAR GNAT

Blue Steel therefore continued as a component of the British nuclear forces until the first of the Polaris-carrying submarines entered service in 1967, and they were finally withdrawn two years later, having in the meantime been modified to permit low-altitude launch in order to defeat—or at least render less effective—Soviet bloc radar systems.

Aeronautical research never stands still, however, and the proven stability of the Vulcan as a heavyweight launch vehicle prompted a number of alternative studies into possible roles for the aircraft, including a dedicated photo-reconnaissance variant, several extended-range versions with additonal fuel in nacelles or in an enlarged fiuselage spine, and a B-2 variant specially equipped to carry six Martel air-to-surface missiles. Amongst the most intriguing, and with the smack of last-ditch World War II Luftwaffe designs, was a bizarre idea involving the carriage of three manned Folland Gnat fighters, each armed with a small nuclear weapon. It was not revealed how the pilots might return safely.

DEAD-ENDS

FINALE

BY 1969, with the Royal Navy's assumption of responsibility for the British 'nuclear deterrent', as it was styled, the Royal Air Force's Vulcans, which had already (circa 1964) been switched to low-level operations rather than high-altitude attack in order to defeat—or, at least, reduce the value of—Soviet ground based radars, were ready for their new task as tactical bombers, armed with either conventional or nuclear weapons. By this time Vulcan production had ended, and those B.1s remaining in service were being withdrawn, having earlier been upgraded to B.1A standard, with revised electronics and countermeasures apparatus, manifested externally by the B.2-type tail fairing and the flat ECM plate between the two engine fairings beneath the mainplane on the starboard side.

The switch to low-level operations emphasised the Vulcan's versatility: this sort of role had not been envisaged twenty years earlier when the blueprints were being prepared, and although low-speed handling had exercised the minds of the aircraft's designers, this was more to do with safe landing approaches than extended operations. Its V-bomber companion the Victor was also employed at low level, but the aircraft was deemed insufficiently strong to assume such a role permanently, its structure being vulnerable to the turbulent air currents encountered during such operations. Outwardly, the Vulcan's physiognomy was virtually indistinguishable from earlier days, although a small dome on the extreme nose indicated the fitting of General Dynamics terrain-following radar (TFR); somewhat earlier, a refuelling probe had been fitted to enable the aircraft's range to be extended. The Blue Saga passive warning system was replaced by RWR radar, for which

Left, upper: XH558 was one of eight Vulcans earmarked for duty as Maritime Radar Reconnaissance aircraft, assigned to No 27 Squadron from 1973 to 1983 as strategic reconnaissance Victors were withdrawn for conversion to tankers. They often carried air sampler pods, and had no TFR 'thimble'. B Mk 2(MRR)s, as the aircraft were designated, carried a high-gloss finish to give extra protection to the paintwork in the salt-laden environment in which they worked. *D. W. Robinson via Richard L. Ward*

Left, lower: The 'sniffer' pods were converted from old Sea Vixen drop tanks. This aircraft features two 'blisters' under each wing outboard of the main undercarriage bays—front spar mounting points for the pylons that would have carried the Skybolt missile. *D. W. Robinson via Richard L. Ward*

Right: B Mk 2(MRR) XH534, up from Scampton, over the North Sea in August 1976. The odd tonal renderings are probably explained by the use of orthochromatic paper in the printing of a colour negative, and the graininess of the original print is no doubt due to the long range from which the photograph was taken. *Peter Stevenson/MoD via Richard L. Ward*

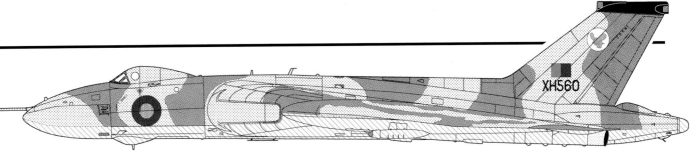

Above: The B Mk 2(MRR)s were painted in Medium Sea Grey and Dark Green camouflage but with Light Aircraft Grey undersurfaces. The Squadron emblem had evolved somewhat since early Vulcan days, 'Dumbo' (by permission of the Walt Disney organisation) having replaced the more austere elephant design shown elsewhere in this book. The nose of the aircraft carries a triangular blade antenna unique to the MRR version of the Vulcan.

the tailfin received a box-like fairing at its tip. Internal changes were similarly subdued, but included new attachment points and lines for the bomb-bay fuel tanks.

MRR

The mid-1970s saw another role for the Vulcan as the ex-V-bomber Victor SR Mk 2 strategic reconnaissance aircraft were withdrawn from service, some earmarked for conversion to flight-refuelling tankers. With the TFR deleted and LORAN navigational aids added, nine B Mk 2s were returned to service as long-range MRR (Maritime Radar Reconnaissance) variants; five of these were adapted specifically to carry underwing air-sampling 'sniffer' pods.

By this time it had been determined that the Vulcan would be phased out, to be 'replaced' by the Panavia Tornado. In truth, of course, the RAF's strategic bombing capability, which had remained one of the service's cornerstones since it came into existence, was being abandoned: while it is undeniably an excellent aircraft, the Tornado, unrefuelled, can take its several tons of destruction less than a fifth the distance than could a Vulcan. The change was nothing less than a fundamental *volte-face* in defence

FINALE 15

policy by the British Government—and its significance would be brought home with a vengeance within a few short years.

LAST ORDERS

Just as the Vulcan was taking its leave of the RAF—and at a time when only a handful of these unique aircraft were still on charge—the Argentine *junta* decided to invade the Falkland Islands, a British Dependent Territory. In Britain, the Thatcher administration was galvanised into immediate action as a result of this affront to British sovereignty, and a naval task force was quickly assembled and despatched to the South Atlantic. Concurrently, Vulcan personnel, at RAF Waddington, where the last few bombers were based, were ordered to prepare for action.

Ten aircraft had their refuelling capability, unused since the switch to low-level tactical operations, refurbished and

Above: Where the goods are stored. Here, the rear third of the bomb bay is occupied by a fuel tank (installed to counteract the CG shift after the refuelling equipment etc had been removed from the nose—and almost certainly never filled!). This is XH558, which in response to public demand was kept flying by the RAF after the Vulcan had been withdrawn from service. *Richard L. Ward*
Left: XM597 rests at RAF Waddington after the Falklands War. Immediately beyond, with just the nose visible, is another combat veteran, XM607. The non-standard Dark Sea Grey undersurfaces are evident.
Below: XM607 carried out three bombing raids—'Black Buck 1', '2' and '7'—over the Falklands, pounding Port Stanley airfield and its environs. The visits were recorded appropriately on the airframe.

a new INS added, and five of them were made ready for immediate conventional bombing operations. All had in previous years been modified to accept the Skybolt missile, and were thus very readily adaptable to the carriage of external stores. Training intensified, extemporary underwing pylons were fabricated and fitted, an AN/ALQ 101 ECM pod was installed beneath the starboard wing, and within a few weeks two aircraft, XM598 and XM607, were en route to Ascension Island in the South Atlantic.

BLACK BUCK

By the early hours of 1 May 1982, and with a complex refuelling pattern involving Victor tankers in place, forty-two 1,000lb bombs were in the air destined for the Falklands and the airfield at Port Stanley. XM598 was forced to abort the mission, but '607 planted a string of bombs across the main runway. This first 'Black Buck' attack was as much symbolic as physically effective: it was brought home to the Argentines that what had happened at Port Stanley could also happen at Buenos Aires, and deployments to the Falklands were reassessed with a view to strengthen-

Below: Wideawake Vulcans: two 'Black Buck' aircraft on Ascension Island, from where the raids over Port Stanley airfield would be conducted. *Mel James via Paul Hartley*

Below: XM597 after the Falklands War. The No 101 Squadron emblem was painted over for combat purposes; so, too was the City of Lincoln shield, although this was subsequently reinstated. The Red Steer radome has been changed from that fitted in 1982, and has different paintwork.

ing homeland air defences, thereby relieving pressure on the British forces in the South Atlantic.

Following a second raid by '607 a few days later, which, however, achieved less success, attention was now directed towards neutralising the enemy radar systems which had been set up on the Falklands. Trials with the AS.37 Martel were carried out, but in the event the US AGM-45 Shrike missile was selected and two raids, again supported by a complex flight-refuelling programme, were made, involving XM597. Both were successful, although the return flight during the second mission had to be hastily replanned when the flight refuelling probe became damaged: unable to receive 'juice' from the Victor tankers, the aircraft was obliged to touch down at Rio de Janeiro, where it was impounded for a week.

XM607 made one further bombing raid over Port Stanley on 11 June, but with the close of hostilities three days later the Vulcan crews were stood down and the aircraft at Ascension returned to Britain. The RAF's long-range bombing option was finally closed off at the end of the year. The operational career of the Vulcan, which right at the end had seen the aircraft go into action, was over. Well, almost.

HOODOO

The long haul down to the South Atlantic, to assist in the rebuilding of the Falklands after hostilities and to keep the garrison stationed there resupplied, had made one fact obvious: there was a dire need for more tanker aircraft. The existing Victors were overworked, and the new VC10 tanker fleet would take some while to be completed, so as an interim measure it was decided to equip a handful of Vulcans to undertake the role. In that true and endearing British tradition, which often results in ingenious lash-ups coming to the rescue of indistinct thinking or parsimony on the part of politicians responsible for the defence of the nation, six Vulcans were taken back to the BAe facility at Woodford (where the aircraft had originally been built some twenty-odd years before) to have five-foot-six-inch wide Hose Drum Units (HDUs, or 'Hoodoos') fitted through four-foot-wide access panels in the aircraft's tail ECM bays and

Top: XM597 delivered two Shrike attacks during the Falklands conflict and recorded the visits appropriately, along with a reminder of the aircraft's unscheduled sojourn in Buenos Aires.

Above: Tanker conversion XL445 taxies for take-off at RAF Waddington.
Below: Tanker B.2K XM571, pouring smoke and revealing a differing paint scheme, receives guidance, February 1984.

18 VULCAN

Above: Fitting a Mk 17B HDU into XH560. It took BAe technicians just a few weeks to get a tanker conversion into the air. *BAe via Paul Hartley*

Below: XH558 was retained by the MoD as the so-called 'Vulcan Display Flight' up to March 1993. The City of Lincoln shield and a Union flag adorn the fin, while the No 1 Group panther embellishes the nose. *BAe*

connected up to three 8,000lb (= 1,000-gallon) capacity tanks in the bomb bays. The external HDU container, looking for all the world like a glorified soap box with traffic lights, was hardly aerodynamic, but, predictably, the whole system worked like magic and the converted aircraft performed valuable service up to March 1984. Thereupon the last remaining heavy bombers in the Royal Air Force ceased operations for good.

One aircraft, XH558, was retained as an airworthy display Vulcan and continued to delight aviation fans for some years until, citing the costs of refurbishing the aircraft and of repeatedly filling its tanks with fuel, the Ministry of Defence announced that it was being put up for sale. A farewell tour was made on 23 March 1993, at the end of which the aircraft returned to Waddington for a final flypast and then departed for Bruntingthorpe and private ownership.

SQUADRONS

DELIVERIES of Vulcan B Mk 1s began in early 1957 when two aircraft were taken on permament charge by No 230 Operational Conversion Unit at RAF Waddington in Lincolnshire. The first front-line unit to receive the new bomber was No 83 Squadron, in July 1957, followed a few months later by No 101, at Finningley, Yorkshire. No 617 Squadron, based at RAF Scampton in Lincolnshire, began to receive B.1s in 1958; by the end of 1961 Nos 83 and 617 had re-equipped with Mk 2s and No 27 had re-formed with the new variant at Scampton, No 83's B.1s being transferred to No 44 Squadron and No 617's going to make up No 50 Squadron. The following year, Nos IX, 12 and 35 Squadrons had re-formed with B Mk 2s at RAF Coningsby, moving in late 1964 to Cottesmore. By 1965, therefore, there were three Vulcan Wings, each composed of three squadrons—a B.1A Wing at Waddington, a Blue Steel B.2 Wing at Scampton and a free-fall B.2 Wing at Cottesmore. No 230 OCU, based at Finningley, had one flight of B.1/1As and one of B.2s. As Blue Steel was phased out, the aircraft returned to the free-fall role.

In the mid-1970s, No 27 Squadron began to operate modified B Mk 2(MRR) maritime radar reconnaissance aircraft, but during 1981–82 the Vulcan squadrons were all expected to be disbanded in favour of re-equipment with Tornados (see AEROGUIDE 24). However, the South Atlantic War in the spring of 1982 brought about an abrupt change of plan, and the three units in being at that time—Nos 44, 50 and 101 Squadrons, based at Waddington—were kept operational. No 50 Squadron continued to fly Vulcans until March 1984, using six aircraft modified as inflight-refuelling tankers (B Mk 2K).

ROYAL AIR FORCE VULCAN SQUADRONS

Unit	Base	Mark(s)	Dates	Remarks
No 230 OCU	Waddington	B.1/1A, B.2	May 1956–Jun 1962	First B.1 course Jan 1957; first B.2 1 Jul 1960.
	Finningley	B.1/1A, B.2	Jun 1962–Dec 1969	B.1/1A retired by Nov 1965.
	Scampton	B.2(FF)	Dec 1969–Aug 1981	
No 83 Squadron	Waddington	B.1	May 1957–Aug 1960	First B.1 squadron. Aircraft to No 44(R) Squadron.
	Scampton	B.2(FF)/(BS)	Oct 1960–Aug 1969	First B.2 squadron. Blue Steel from Aug 1962.
No 101 Squadron	Finningley	B.1	Oct 1957–Jun 1961	
	Waddington	B.1/1A, B.2	Jun 1961–Aug 1982	First squadron to train for low-level operations (Jul 1963). Re-equipped with B.2 from Oct 1967.
No 617 Squadron	Scampton	B.1/1A	May 1958–Aug 1961	Aircraft disposed to No 50 Sqn.
	Scampton	B.2(BS)/(FF)	Sep 1961–Dec 1981	First Blue Steel squadron (B.1/1As to No 50 Squadron). Last Blue Steel sortie Dec 1970.
No 44(R) Squadron	Waddington	B.1/1A, B.2(FF)	Aug 1960–Dec 1982	B.1s from No 83 Squadron. Last Vulcan bomber squadron.
No 27 Squadron	Scampton	B.2(FF)/(BS)	Apr 1961–Mar 1972	Blue Steel Nov 1962–Dec 1969.
	Scampton	B.2(MRR)	Nov 1973–Mar 1982	Also operated some standard B.2s.
No 50 Squadron	Waddington	B.1/1A, B.2/2K	Aug 1961–Mar 1984	B.1/1As from No 617 Squadron. All three B.1/1A squadrons now at Waddington. Converted to B.2 Dec 1965–Jul 1966. B.2K from Jun 1982.
No IX Squadron	Coningsby	B.2(FF)	Mar 1962–Nov 1964	Second B.2 Wing forming at Coningsby, with aircraft from Nos 27 and 83 Squadrons.
	Cottesmore	B.2(FF)	Nov 1964–Feb 1969	301-engined aircraft to Waddington 1967 on, re-equipping with latter's 200-series aircraft.
	Akrotiri	B.2(FF)	Feb 1969–Jan 1975	Near East Air Force Bomber Wing.
	Waddington	B.2(FF)	Jan 1975–Apr 1982	
No 12 Squadron	Coningsby	B.2(FF)	Jul 1962–Nov 1964	Formed with aircraft from Nos 27 and 83 Squadrons.
	Cottesmore	B.2(FF)	Nov 1964–Dec 1967	Spare Cottesmore Wing aircraft to Waddington to replace B.1As.
No 35 Squadron	Coningsby	B.2(FF)	Dec 1962–Nov 1964	Formed with aircraft from Nos 27 and 83 Squadrons.
	Cottesmore	B.2(FF)	Nov 1964–Feb 1969	301-engined aircraft to Waddington 1967 on, re-equipping with latter's 200-series aircraft.
	Akrotiri	B.2(FF)	Feb 1969–Jan 1975	Near East Air Force Bomber Wing.
	Scampton	B.2(FF)	Jan 1975–Apr 1982	On disbandment, some aircraft to Waddington.

20 VULCAN

Top: Air brakes raised and lowered, a No 27 Squadron Vulcan touches down. The Squadron Commander's pennant is carried just behind the roundel. *Flight International via Richard L. Ward*

Above: An Akrotiri Wing Vulcan, March 1973. Unusually, XL446 has 'tactical' (red/blue) roundels yet retains white under-surfaces and a overall glossy finish. *Carmel J. Attard*

Right: B.2s of No 50 Squadron await their turn for conversion into tanker aircraft, May 1982. XH561, the first to be returned to service, is nearest the camera; this aircraft features prominently in the close-up views later in this book. The other Vulcans in the picture are XJ825 and XM573. *BAe via Paul Hartley*

PAINTWORK

ALTHOUGH some early development and OCU Vulcans were aluminium overall in appearance, in squadron service the B Mk 1s had glossy white paintwork, which was more effective in reflecting the heat of a nuclear detonation should the aircraft ever be called upon to go to war. On some B Mk 1As late in their careers, and on B Mk 2s as they were delivered, the red and blue elements of the national markings on wings, fuselage and tail were reduced in intensity and appeared as pale pink and pale blue, respectively. Fin serial numbers were painted in the same pale blue, and airframe stencilling and squadron markings were also subdued; underwing serial numbers, previously black on B.1s, were deleted altogether. (For the same reason, this general scheme was adopted also by the Valiant and Victor strategic bombers—although in the case of the former the national markings were not modified—and also, briefly, by the Buccaneer S Mk 1 and the ill-fated TSR.2.)

Above: The bat emblem in the Squadron crest reveals the ownership of this early Vulcan (XL385)—No IX Squadron, based at RAF Coningsby in summer 1963. The listing of crew names on the exterior of Vulcans was distinctly unusual, to say the least. The pale hues of the roundel and airframe instructional notices are well shown here. *J. D. R. Rawlings via Richard L. Ward*

DISRUPTIVE SCHEMES

With the switch to low-level operations in the mid-1960s, and the consequent requirement to reduce the visibility of the aircraft from above, Vulcans began to receive disruptive camouflage on their uppersurfaces, using Dark Green and Medium Sea Grey paint. For the time being, the lower surfaces remained white (anti-flash) and national markings red, white and blue, although to reduce symmetry the wing roundel was applied to the port side only. Serial numbers, in the standard height of 18in for Vulcans, were black, and

Below: Standard B Mk 2 from No 12 Squadron, based at RAF Coningsby in 1963 and in anti-flash finish. The unit's fox emblem on the fin is medium brown with a white outline and black detail. *Author*

Below: A similar scheme for a Mk 2A, with the triple lightning flashes carried by No 617 Squadron matching the pink of the national markings. RAF Scampton, 1963.

Below: Another Blue Steel Vulcan, a similar scheme: No 27 Squadron, RAF Scampton, 1962–63. The elephant design is dark green.

22 VULCAN

Above left: With the coming of camouflage, roundels were repainted as standard Type 'Ds'. This aircraft has its nose camouflage line following, in part, the angular break of the radome. *Richard L. Ward*

Above right: Toning down: Light Aircraft Grey undersides and two-tone roundels. XL317 of No 617 Squadron, 1978, also has 'soft' camouflage edges. *Richard L. Ward*

the overall finish was usually glossy polyurethane, which both protected the paintwork and gave a few extra knots of speed. The forward section of the nose radome, and the fin tip, were finished in black, as they had been from the beginning of the Vulcan's service, but at this time squadron insignia were generally not carried on the fin, owing to the policy of Centralised Servicing, wherein air crews remained on individual squadrons but engineering facilties were pooled.

Modifications to this scheme came in the early 1970s with the introduction on some aircraft of Light Aircraft Grey lower surfaces, and the black-painted nose radomes began to disappear as the refuelling probes and then the TFR 'thimbles' were installed. This was also the period when a general 'toning-down' of national insignia came into effect: roundels and fin flashes were finished in red and blue only, with red half the diameter of the

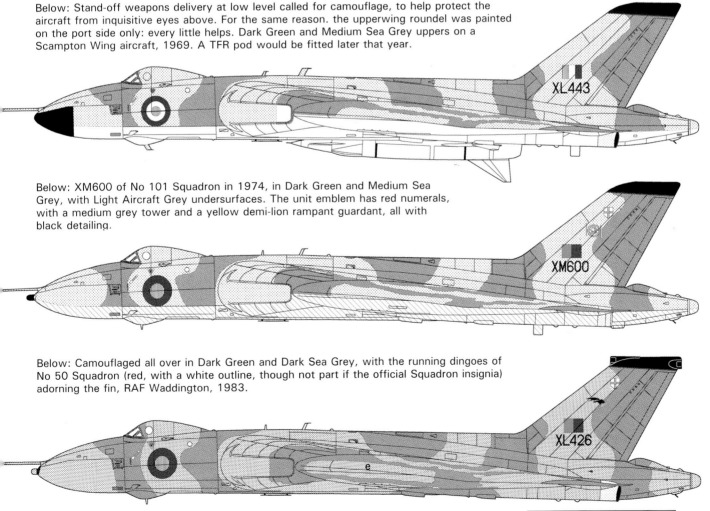

Below: Stand-off weapons delivery at low level called for camouflage, to help protect the aircraft from inquisitive eyes above. For the same reason. the upperwing roundel was painted on the port side only: every little helps. Dark Green and Medium Sea Grey uppers on a Scampton Wing aircraft, 1969. A TFR pod would be fitted later that year.

Below: XM600 of No 101 Squadron in 1974, in Dark Green and Medium Sea Grey, with Light Aircraft Grey undersurfaces. The unit emblem has red numerals, with a medium grey tower and a yellow demi-lion rampant guardant, all with black detailing.

Below: Camouflaged all over in Dark Green and Dark Sea Grey, with the running dingoes of No 50 Squadron (red, with a white outline, though not part if the official Squadron insignia) adorning the fin, RAF Waddington, 1983.

PAINTWORK 23

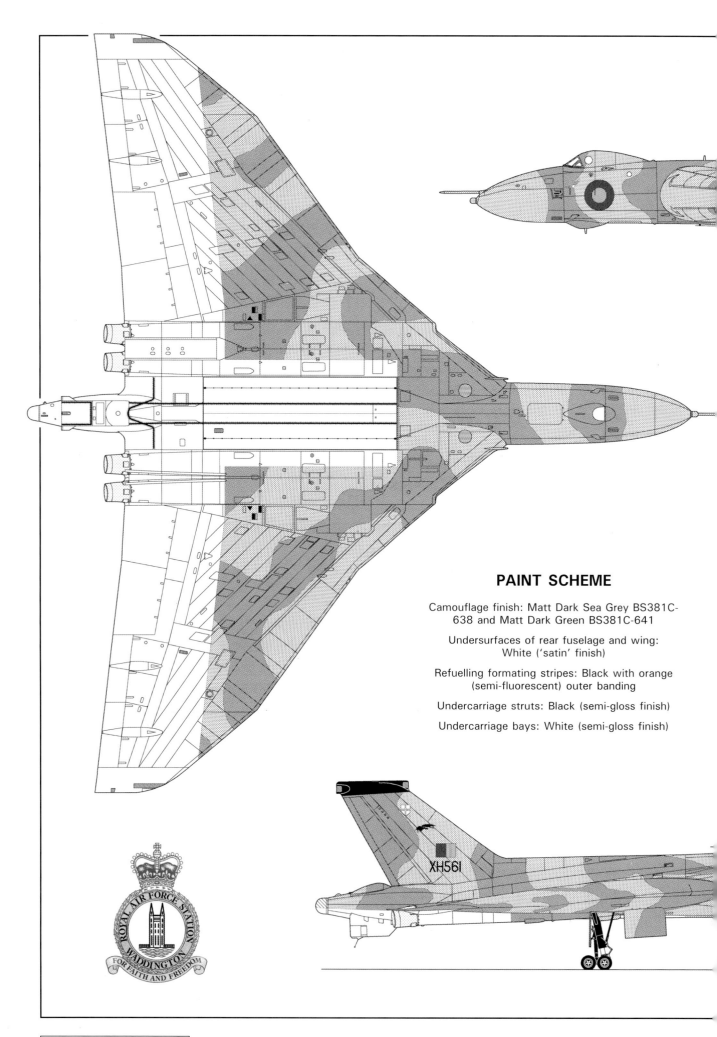

PAINT SCHEME

Camouflage finish: Matt Dark Sea Grey BS381C-638 and Matt Dark Green BS381C-641

Undersurfaces of rear fuselage and wing: White ('satin' finish)

Refuelling formating stripes: Black with orange (semi-fluorescent) outer banding

Undercarriage struts: Black (semi-gloss finish)

Undercarriage bays: White (semi-gloss finish)

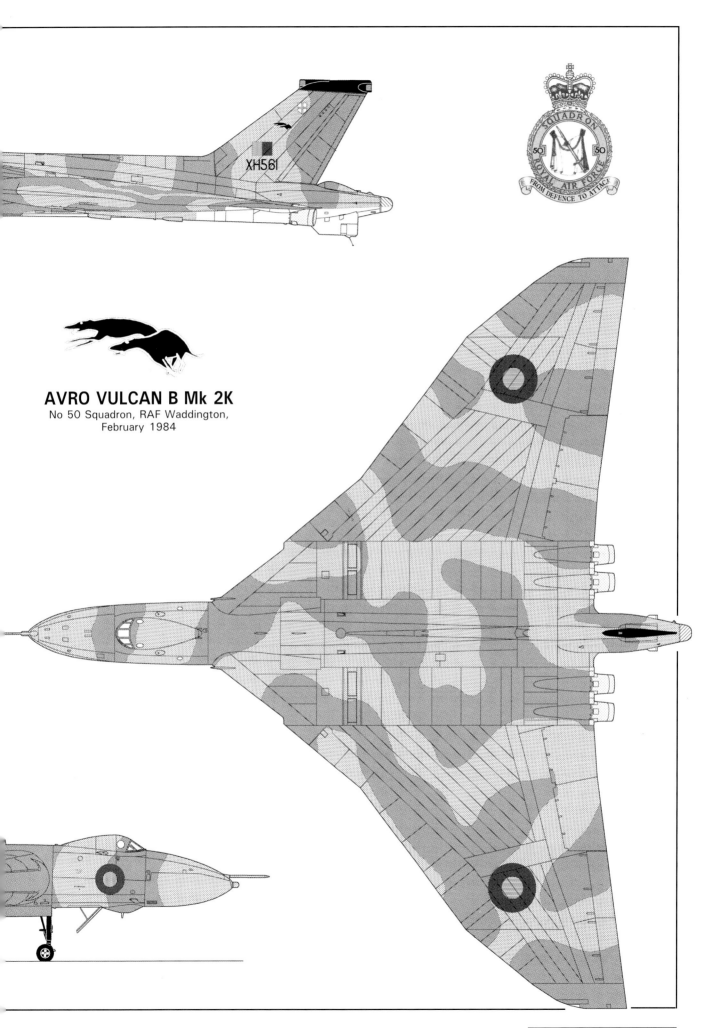

AVRO VULCAN B Mk 2K
No 50 Squadron, RAF Waddington,
February 1984

roundel. Sizes remained constant at 84in for the wing and 54in for the fuselage, with a 36in × 24in fin flash. Generally, though not invariably, the camouflaged paintwork was taken across and below the central datum of the wing leading edge and, similarly, along and below the lower rims of the main intakes. The upperwing roundel reappeared on the starboard side.

Towards the end of the Vulcan's service, disruptive camouflage in matt (or 'satin') Dark Green and Dark Sea Grey was applied to the entire airframe; loosely speaking, the undersurfaces were schemed as a mirror image of the uppersurface pattern. The low-visibility 'tactical' type national markings were retained, but wing serial numbers were still absent. In 1977, two aircraft received disruptive 'desert' camouflage (sand and stone)

Above: Head-on to a camouflaged B.2, showing the extent to which the upper paintwork 'wrapped' the wing leading edges and intakes. *Richard L. Ward*
Below (clockwise from top left): Tail decor for Nos 35, 44, 35 again and 101 Squadrons. *Richard L. Ward*

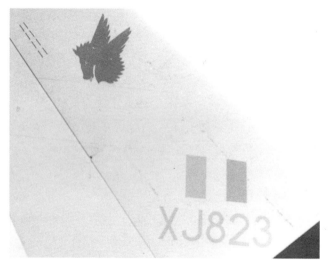

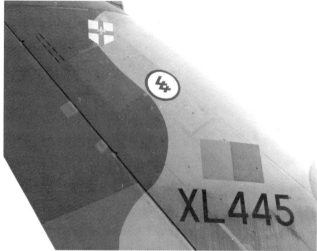

Above: A none-too-sharp but nevertheless unusual image of a Blue Steel Vulcan B.2 of No 617 Squadron touching down, late 1963. *D. W. Robinson via Richard L. Ward*
Below (clockwise from top left): Tail decor for Nos 617, 35 (variation), IX and 27 Squadrons. No 27 later adopted 'Dumbo'—see page 39. *Richard L. Ward*

on the undersurfaces for the 'Red Flag' event in the United States. In 1982, the Falklands War participants had their undersides painted matt Dark Sea Grey.

The Vulcan B Mk 2K tankers of No 50 Squadron had their paint scheme modified in order to assist 'prods': as shown in the drawings on pages 24 and 25, although the disruptive grey and green camouflage or plain Light Aircraft Grey still extended across the lower surfaces of the aircraft, the undersides of the fuselage as far forward as the front of the bomb bay and the after fifty per cent of the undersides of the wings were finished in glossy white, and high-visibility longitudinal striping in black and semi-luminous ('Dayglo'-type) orange was added to help receiving pilots align their aircraft correctly. National markings continued to be displayed in red and blue only.

Avro Vulcan B Mk 2 No IX Squadron, RAF Coningsby, 1963

Avro Vulcan B Mk 2 No 83 Squadron, RAF Scampton, 1963

Avro Vulcan B Mk 2 No 617 Squadron, RAF Cottesmore, Spring 1975

Avro Vulcan B Mk 2 'Black Buck', Operation 'Corporate', May/June 1982

Right: Before the fame: XM597 in the first Vulcan camouflage scheme of Medium Sea Grey and Dark Green, with white under-surfaces and 'D' type roundels, photographed in the mid-1970s. The only fin emblem is the City of Lincoln shield. *Richard L. Ward*

Below: XL444 of No 617 Squadron up from Scampton on a low-level training flight in the north of England and in spanking new paintwork, late 1975. The fin-top RWR equipment is not fitted. The scheme worn by this aircraft a few months before this photograph was taken is depicted on pages 28–29. *Andy Leitch.*

Bottom: XM575 in full wraparound camouflage and low-visibility markings, except for the No 44 Squadron emblem and City of Lincoln shield on the fin. The airfield beneath is RAF Waddington: the dispersed Vulcans display both Medium Sea Grey and Dark Sea Grey in their paint schemes. *BAe*

Right: Camouflage patterns were generally similar amongst Vulcans, but not identical, as can be seen when comparing this image with that opposite. Here, XM650 of No 50 Squadron, circa 1980, also seems to display variations in the shade of Medium Sea Grey. *Richard L. Ward*

Below: Falklands veteran XM607 during her final days at RAF Waddington, the No 44 Squadron badge restored. *Richard L. Ward*

Bottom: XM606—here with white 'bib', Union flag on the fin and No 1 Group's panther behind the fuselage roundel—last served with No IX Squadron before being presented to the US Air Force after the Falklands War. See page 22 for an earlier incarnation. *BAe*

UP CLOSE

Above: Early-morning frost recedes from the nose of Vulcan B Mk 2K XH561, February 1984. The fairing alongside the cockpit canopy houses a sextant mounting (and is duplicated on the port side). Further aft is the observation port.
Right: Terrain-following radar was added to the Vulcan's nose when the aircraft were switched to low-level bombing operations. The pod itself is considerably longer than the exterior dome suggests, most of it being carried within the airframe. Refuelling probes appeared on the aircraft a little earlier. Exterior colours on both fittings varied.
Below: The tip of the nose from the starboard side. Again, that's frost, not camouflage!

Right, top: A smart Vulcan in the early (glossy) camouflage scheme. The crew entrance door is lowered, and, forward of this, the bomb-aimer's blister and flat panel are readily identifiable.
Richard L. Ward
Right, upper: An overhead view of the canopy glazing.
Paul Hartley
Far right, upper: XM597's bomb-aimer's fairing, with UHF antenna beneath.
Right, lower: Crew entrance hatch and nose undercarriage gear.
Far right, lower: Pitot head and tacan blade, above the starboard nosewheel door.

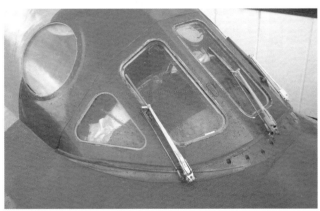

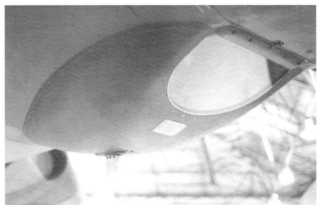

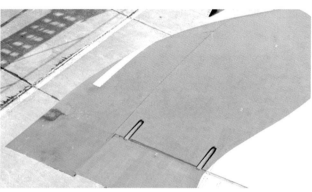

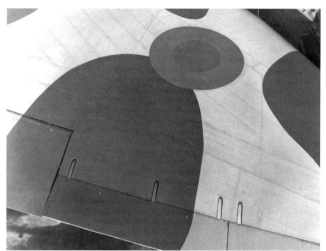

The vast expanse of the Vulcan's wing. Panel lines are prominent and rivet heads can be detected, as can the numerous hoist symbols; visible, too, are interesting small details such as the 'No step' symbols *within* cooling intakes. Camouflage boundaries here are, typically, hard-edged (though Vulcans appearing in sprayed finishes were not uncommon). The outlines of the upperwing airbrakes can be traced—the exterior paintwork on each brake unit has darkened noticeably—with warning stripes in yellow either side along with some local oil streaks. UHF and VHF (communications) and IFF antennas (from front to rear, with the VHF blade and the IFF offset to port) are visible on the fuselage top, with the radio compass loop panel further aft and various other dielectric panels towards the base of the fin. The anti-collision light can be made out, with the rectangular bomb bay air-conditioning inlets nearby. Aircraft XH561 has received replacement elevons, resulting in a mismatch of the camouflage pattern—see page 39 for a colour view of the aircraft which better illustrates the local variations in paint shades.

34 VULCAN

Undersurface physiognomy: at left the photographs depict a Mk 2K tanker; at right, the top two an aircraft in the early, glossy camouflage scheme with white undersurfaces; then a Vulcan camouflaged overall; and finally, bottom, a view under the starboard wing of a B Mk 2K, the giveaway being the sharp latitudinal undersurface paint boundary. Pre-flight activities are taking place around XH561 (left). The Olympus engines were accessed from below via numerous panels, and were of course also removed from below for major servicing and changing. The white undersurfaces of the Vulcan pictured top right are remarkably clean: as can be seen from illustrations elsewhere in this book, oil streaking and other deposits quickly made a mess of the engine panelling during flying operations. The lens of the starboard landing light can be seen in the photograph bottom right, just forward of the break line in the paint scheme. *Top three photographs page 37: Richard L. Ward*

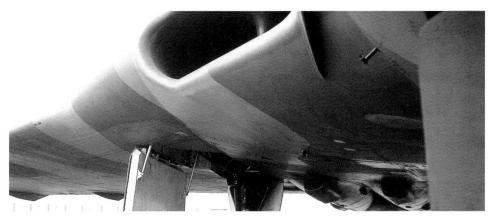

38 VULCAN

Opposite upper: Tails of two Vulcans. XM603, here in 1996, was returned to Avro (now BAe Systems, Woodford) in March 1982 and served as the mock-up for the tanker conversions. The aircraft remains there under preservation. XL385, shown here in the markings of No IX Squadron in 1963, was one of the last seven 200-series-engined aircraft delivered to the RAF. Quite soon after this photograph was taken, it was returned to Avro and given Blue Steel modifications, a refuelling probe and camouflage and issued to the Scampton Wing. *Richard L. Ward*

Opposite lower: Starboard side of the tail fairing. The tanker conversions had the characteristic (but now redundant) cooling intake removed.

Above: Last-minute pre-flight adjustments for XH561.

Below: The fin-top modification applied to Vulcans from the mid-1970s onwards was to accommodate ARI.18228 radar warning receivers (RWR), which were retrofitted to virtually all RAF combat aircraft during this period and are nowadays standard equipment; on Vulcans, the equipment replaced the earlier Blue Saga. Installed atop the tail fairing is the brake parachute housing. This is a B.2(MRR) from No 27 Squadron, RAF Scampton. *Richard L. Ward*

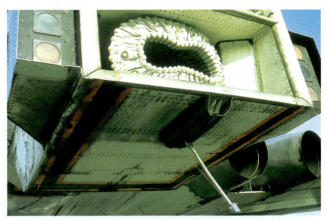

Opposite top left: Rearward-looking 'Red Steer' X-band radar was carried by all Vulcan B.2s. This is XH561 with the Mk 2 dome — although, being a tanker, the aircraft would have had the radar itself removed. The earlier Mk 1 dome was rather more squat, as can be seen, for example, in the photograph of XH558 on page 39. British weapons projects, both offensive and defensive, have for long been given names prefixed with a colour reference.

Opposite top right: The cooling intake for the tail-mounted ECM equipment bay was situated on the starboard side of the standard B Mk 2, complete with warning stripes and 'No Step' symbol.

Opposite centre: Four views of the tanker's HDU ('Hoo-doo', or 'skip'). The drogue basket deployed aerodynamically but was reeled in after use by an electro-hydraulic motor. The 'ready' lights on either side of the skip — amber at the top, green and red — were complemented by a forward-facing spotlight on each side to illuminate the undersides of the aircraft during nocturnal 'prods'. Beneath the skip is the tail-down sensor: rotation on take off and landing had to be monitored more carefully than usual with the tankers, owing to reduced ground clearance. What the Avro aerodynamicists of the early 1950s thought of this contraption bolted on to their beautiful design can of course only be imagined.

Opposite bottom: Black and semi-fluorescent orange stripes aided the receiving pilot as he lined up for a 'drink'.

Right: The main intakes. Apart from the first ten production aircraft, Mk 2s had deeper intakes (in terms of the top-to-bottom dimension) than Mk 1s, to allow an enhanced airflow for the more powerful Olympus 301 engines. The smaller intake inboard of the boundary layer splitter plate can be seen in the third photograph. In these views, red-painted intake blanks are present, to guard against FOD (foreign object damage); and the differing paintwork on the interior surfaces of the intakes can be compared.

This page: The first Vulcan B Mk 2s off the production lines were fitted with four 17,000lb thrust Bristol Siddeley Olympus 201 turbojets, but, in order to cope with the demands of the Skybolt missile, later aircraft had 20,000lb 301s installed; the 201s were in due course upgraded to 202s. The tailpipe shroud of the 200-series powerplant was longer and narrower, and tapered noticeably when compared to its uprated counterpart. The illustrations here show 202s, which had a different starting system from the 201s they replaced and could be distinguished externally by the five angular fairings on each nozzle near the junction with the nacelle.
Picture below right: Richard L. Ward

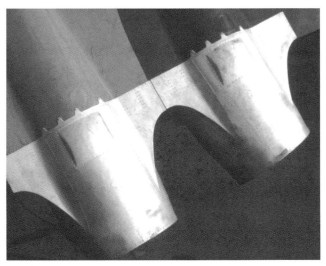

Above left: Inboard wing trailing edge, adjacent to 202 nozzle. All the Vulcan tankers had 200-series powerplants.

Above right: The oil breathers beneath the 202 tailpipes, starboard side, and the mounting pylon for the horizontal plate that, on combat Vulcans, carried electronic countermeasures gear.

Left and below left: The 301 tailpipes, showing how, compared to the 200-series, the exhaust nozzles were shorter and of more or less constant diameter thoughout their length.

Below right: The ECM plate of a B.2, with two Red Shrimp noise jammer 'domes' occupying the forward positions; as shown elsewhere in this book, other arrangements were commonplace, and an L-band jammer was a frequent occupant. The plate generally appeared on the starboard side only, although some Blue Steel Vulcans appear to have had them beneath both pairs of engine fairings.

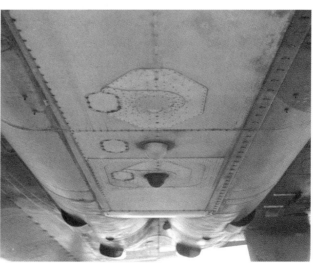

UP CLOSE 43

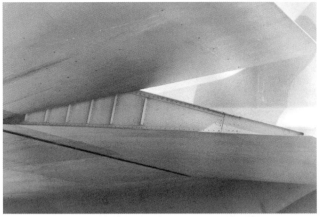

This page: Wing details. The Vulcan B.2's horizontal movable surfaces consisted of combined elevons (the B.1 had ailerons outboard and elevators inboard). The finesse at the trailing edge of the inboard units contrasts noticeably with the rather cast-iron appearance at the trailing edge of the outboard surfaces (above left). The outboard PFCU (powered flying control unit) fairings beneath the wing are shown above right (the inboard units were internal), and the navigation light and dielectric strip for Blue Diver barrage noise jamming equipment at the wing tips can be seen immediately left. The starboard upper airbrake is extended in the image below.

This page: More lumps and bumps, including one of the large vents beneath each engine nacelle, the port-side blisters covering the Skybolt pylon mountings and the the RAT cover below the port main intake (ram air turbine—for providing emergency electrical power). Chaff ('Window') and flare (infra-red decoy) boxes were apparent on XL426 in 1984, aft of the main wheel bays—to combat radar-homing and heat-seeking missiles, respectively; the close-up view is of the flare chutes. The Decca Doppler radar panel (below) was situated under the port wing immediately behind the main wheel bay (the rear door for which is in evidence). At bottom left is the X-band jammer 'tub' under the tail of XM597. The two images bottom right show the tailskid sensor, navigation lamp and outlet grille beneath the Mk 2 tail fairing; and B Mk 2K XH561's fuel dump at the tail (starboard side only).

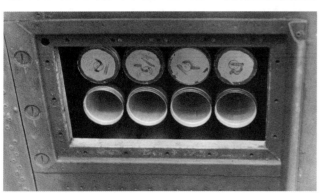

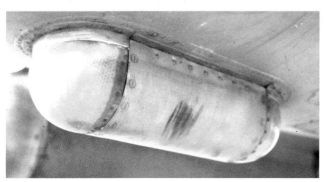

UP CLOSE 45

LANDING GEAR

Above: Nosegear leg and twin wheels. The leg itself is semi-gloss black and the wheel hubs silver; the sheen on the tyres suggests a recent fit. The aircraft's serial number appears along the lower edge of both nosewheel doors. The photograph at right gives a glimpse into the nosewheel bay.
Below left: The port nosegear door of a B Mk 2, showing the radio compass sense aerial (natural metal with red tips).
Below right: A close view of the port main gear, showing the eight-wheel bogie configuration.

Opposite: Further aspects of the main undercarriage units, showing the starboard bogie with its torque links, oleo strut and hydraulic lines; details of one of the cavernous main bays, showing its lock struts, bracing tubes and interior lighting; and, at bottom left, the starboard main wheel door with its operating jacks and, along the bottom edge, locking clips. All three wheel bays of Vulcans were generally finished in semi-gloss white, which gradually took on a yellowish appearance in service.

46 VULCAN

LANDING GEAR 47

INSIDE INFO

This page: The Vulcan had a crew of five — pilot, co-pilot, air electronics officer, nav plotter and nav radar. Shown above is the main instrument panel, with the 'fighter type' control sticks at the base. *(BAe)*. Above right are the pilot's flying instruments and console on the port side of the aircraft *(BAe)*, and immediately right is a detail showing part of the co-pilot's centre panel. The other three crewmen sat facing aft: below left is the nav plotter's station, to starboard of the aircraft; in the centre is the AEO's central position; and at far right is the station for the nav radar (port side of the aircraft). *(BAe)*. The photograph centre right shows the specially fitted instrument panel for the nav radar's refuelling duties in Vulcan tankers, and that far right a detail of the harness fitted to one of the rear-facing crew seats. Only the pilot and co-pilot were supplied with ejection seats (top right) — the Martin Baker Type 3KS *(Martin Baker Aircraft Co)*

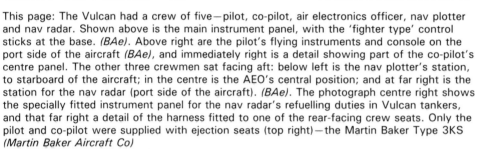

48 VULCAN

INSIDE INFO 49

THE PUNCH

Main picture: A 301-engined Vulcan reveals its *raison d'être*, in a view which also gives a glimpse of the undersurface layout and such add-ons as a pair of Red Shrimps, an L-band jammer and an X-band jammer. *Richard L. Ward*

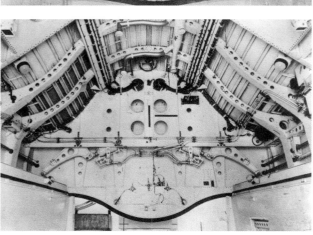

Left, upper: Although the Vulcan was designed for the nuclear role, the aircraft could be readily equipped to carry conventional weapons. The standard load was twenty-one 1,000lb bombs, arranged in racks of seven, as shown. *Bob Downey via Richard L. Ward*
Left, centre and lower: Bomb bay bulkheads—front (above) and rear. The cranked-up front spar, visible in the upper image, had to be configured in this way to accommodate Blue Steel. *BAe*

Right, upper: The bomb bay of a B Mk 2K, showing the three fuel tanks that could be accommodated, each having a capacity of 8,000lb. The usual B.2 fit (in modified aircraft) was either one forward and one aft, or one aft only. *Paul Hartley*

Right, centre and lower: Shrike anti-radiation missiles were fired in earnest during the Falklands War by XM597. Shown here are the twin pylon and launcher under the port wing, and the pylon with the missiles *in situ*. The pylons—which were fabricated at RAF Waddington for the express purpose of the Shrike raids—utilised the mountings that had previously been installed on many aircraft in connection with the abortive Skybolt missile programme. *Bob Downey via Richard L. Ward*

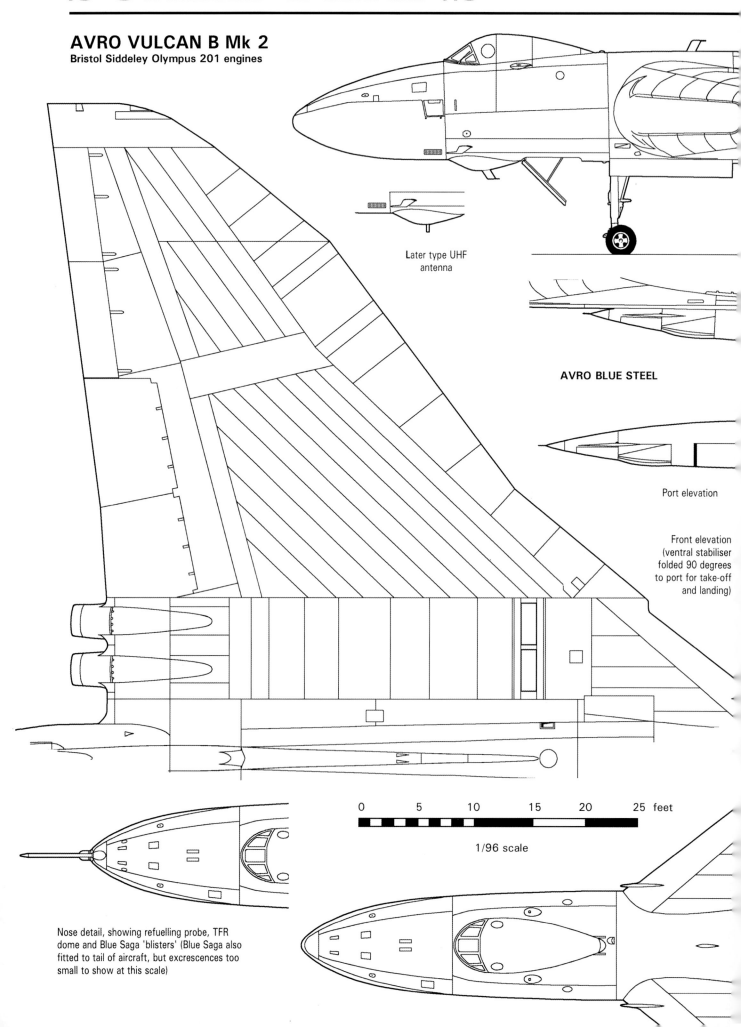

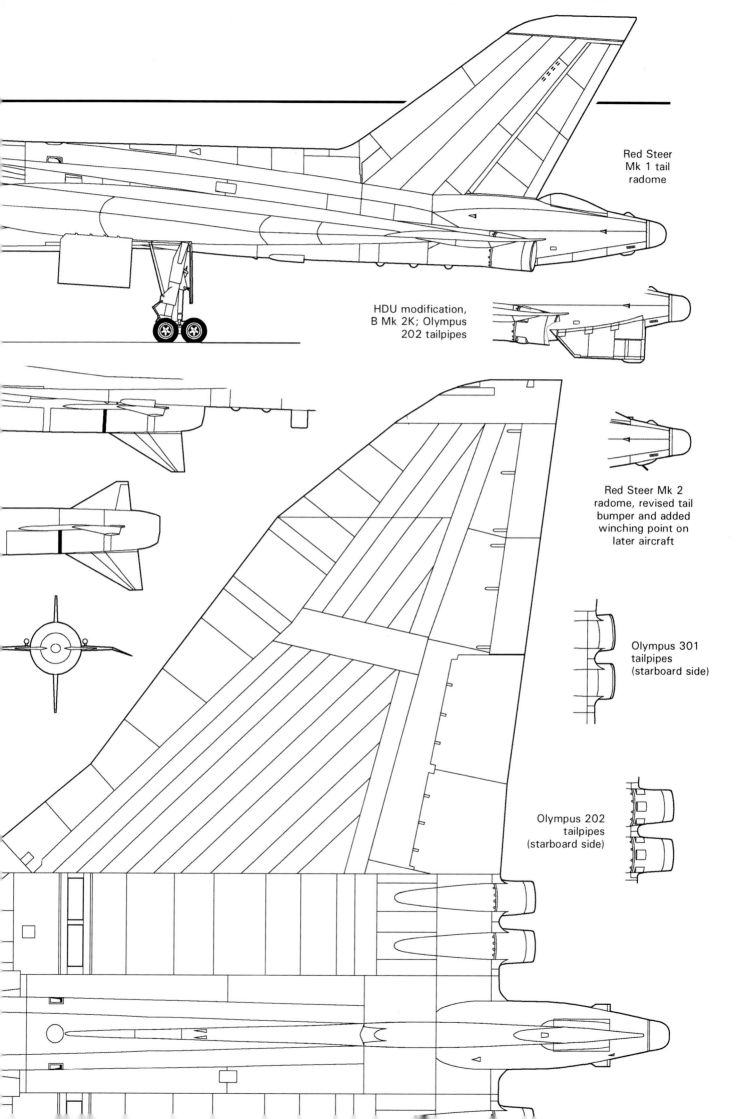

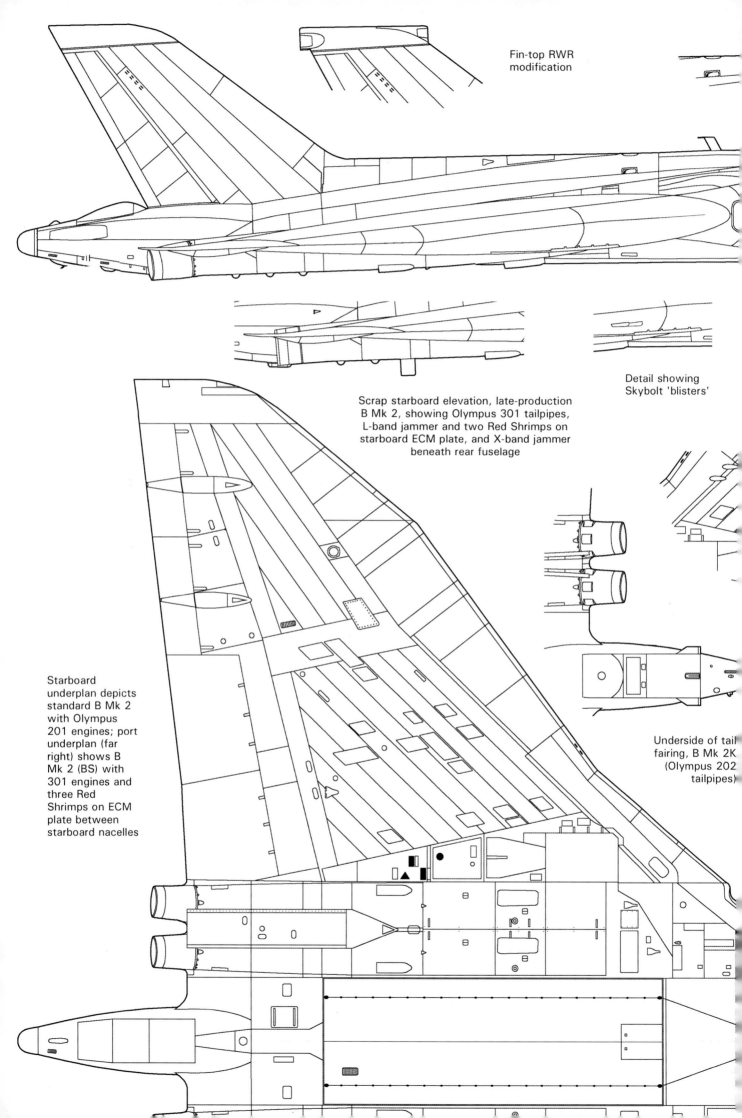

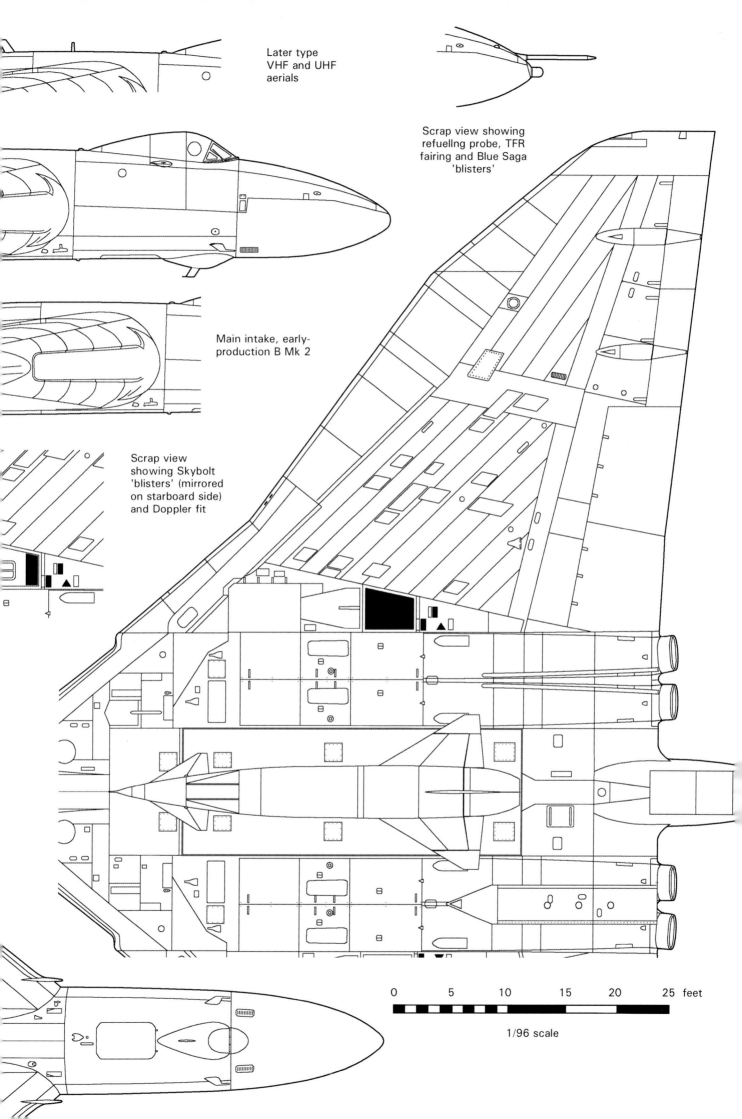

TAIL-END TALK

FOLLOWING the retirement in 1993 of XH558—the first Vulcan B Mk 2 to join the Royal Air Force and the very last one to leave—the aircraft was kept in serviceable condition to the standards set out by the RAF servicing schedule, which included engine ground runs on a 28-day cycle. For six years XH558 performed annual fast taxi demonstrations down Bruntingthorpe's two-mile runway, to the delight of many enthusiasts. During 1999, and after many months of meetings with the Civil Aviation Authority, BAe Systems (the aircraft's design authority) and companies that supported the type with components, it was announced that a full survey on of the aircraft would be undertaken with a view that, provided it were structurally and mechanically sound, it could one day fly again on the civil register.

The survey concluded that the airframe was indeed sound, and that, with eight zero-timed Olympus 201s in store, it would be viable to return a 'Vulcan to the Sky'. The Vulcan Operating Company was formed to oversee the engineering aspect of the project, and a public appeal raised over one-third of the projected £3 million needed to get XH558 airborne. The aircraft was stripped of avionics, engines, landing gear—almost everything that could be removed—and the components were sent to the original equipment manufacturers for refurbishment. It was hoped that the remaining £2 million would be funded by corporate sponsorship, but it soon became apparent that potential sponsors would offer support only if the aircraft were available for flight, and they were reluctant to wait the 12 to 18 months it would take before the aircraft could receive a permit to fly from the CAA.

By late 2001 work had stopped on the restoration, and the aircraft was kept in a 'care and maintenance' programme. In the spring of 2002 an application for a grant of over £2 million was made by The Vulcan Operating Company (subsequently renamed Vulcan To The Sky Ltd) to the Heritage Lottery Fund (HLF), but in November 2002 the application was rejected, one of the reasons cited being that the project was not considered to represent value for money for the British public (!). The decision caused somthing of a public outcry and featured in the national press and on national television. Vulcan To The Sky listened to the comments given by the HLF and reapplied for funding in May 2003. The new application is over 700 pages long and has the support of many influential organisations, including the CAA, BAe Systems and Rolls-Royce, and a decision is pending as these words are written . . .

VULCANS PRESERVED

XH558	The Vulcan Operating Company, Bruntingthorpe, Leicestershire (see above)
XJ823	B Mk 2(MRR) owned by Tom Stoddard; on loan to Solway Aviation Museum, Carlisle
XJ824	Imperial War Museum, Duxford (Blue Steel aircraft)
XL318	Royal Air Force Museum, Hendon
XL319	North-East Aircraft Museum, Sunderland Airport
XL360	Midland Air Museum, Coventry Airport (Blue Steel aircraft)
XL361	RAF Support Unit, Goose Bay (handed over by MoD to Mayor of Happy Valley in recognition of the support given by the town to RAF Goose Bay)
XL391	Manchester Vulcan Bomber Society, Blackpool Airport
XL426	Vulcan Restoration Trust, Southend Airport
XM573	SAC Museum, Offutt AFB
XM575	East Midlands Aeropark, East Midlands Airport, Leicestershire (Blue Steel aircraft)
XM594	Newark Air Museum, Winthorpe, Nottinghamshire
XM597	National Museum of Flight, East Fortune Airfield, Lothian
XM598	Royal Air Force Museum, Cosford
XM603	Avro Heritage Society, BAe Systems, Woodford
XM605	Castle Air Museum, Castle AFB, California
XM606	Eighth Air Force Museum, Barksdale AFB, Louisiana
XM607	RAF Waddington (gate guardian)
XM612	City of Norwich Aviation Museum, Norwich Airport
XM655	655 Maintenance and Preservation Society, Wellesbourne Mountford, Warwickshire (occasional ground runs; charity status applied for)

The foregoing are complete airframes. Several Vulcan sections (e.g. cockpits) are also preserved, and most of these are on public display or can be inspected by appointment. No complete B.1 airframe exists: the last, XA903, was broken up in 1986.